W9-CFX-988

Written by Anne Cotton and Fran Martin

Illustrated by Lyn Hope

It's Almost Christmas Time

Teaching a Theme Using
Whole Language Strategies

Dedication

To teachers and children everywhere
who believe in the magic of language.

Published by
Teaching Resource Center
P.O. Box 1509
San Leandro, CA 94577

Printed in the United States of America
ISBN: 1–56785–012–X

Contents

Theme At A Glance

Trade Books & Big Books

A Christmas Promise
Bah! Humbug?
Boxes! Boxes!
Ed Emberley's Big Red Drawing Book
Fat Santa
Nicky's Christmas Surprise
Santa Mouse
The Cobweb Christmas
The Family Christmas Tree Book
The Gift Of The Magi
The Polar Express
The Twelve Days Of Christmas

A Little House Of Brown
Must Be Santa
What Shall We Put On The
   Christmas Tree?

Class Books & Booklets

ABC Christmas Book
Christmas Tree Strip Book
I Like Christmas Trees
Our Christmas Tree Has...
Reinder Strip Book
The First Gift Of Christmas
The Trap Book

Christmas Sticker Booklet
"Gifts" Booklet
Santa Build-Up Booklet
Santa's Journey Booklet

Songs

Must Be Santa
Sing A Song For Christmas
It's Almost Christmas Time
What Shall We Put On The Christmas Tree?

 # Art

Build A Trap To Catch Santa
Drawing Christmas Trees
Glow In The Dark Tree
Our Twelve Days Of Christmas Bulletin Board

 # Science & Math

Evergreen Tree Facts
Reindeer Facts

Ordinal & Cardinal Numerals
Pattern Block Snowflakes

 # Drama

Bah! Humbug?
Sing A Song For Christmas
The Cobweb Christmas
The Polar Express

The Basic Teaching Strategies

In the development of this theme you will find phrases as **brainstorm for, develop in the pocket chart, sort and classify,** etc. To help clarify these phrases we have listed these basic teaching strategies and have given a brief description of each.

Fill with language:

This is when we read to the children. We read not only stories but poetry and factual information as well. We begin with a discussion of the illustrations to develop as much oral language as possible. We stop periodically to provide the opportunity for the child to anticipate and predict what might happen next. We also read a selection many times over to help make that selection become a part of the child. We feel strongly that we must continually *fill the child with language* as we move ahead with the theme.

Chanting:

Children need to work orally with the patterns of language. The primary way to do this with very young children is by chanting. This technique helps instill the rhythm and structure of language which then becomes a part of their everyday speech.

One way to chant is by using the my turn, your turn technique. The teacher reads a phrase and the children echo this phrase. The teacher tracks (runs hand under the text, pointing to each word) as the chanting takes place. Children may chant using the whole text (pictures, pictures and words, or words alone), or merely chant a repetitive phrase ("Not I," said the dog.) Chanting may be done using big books, charts, brainstorming ideas, pocket chart activities, trade books, etc. Songs and poems should also be included. When working with songs and poetry, we often add rhythmic hand movements which help instill the rhythm of the language and enhances the memorization.

Brainstorming:

Brainstorming is when children orally respond to a question posed by the teacher with the results usually being recorded where they may be seen by the children. This gives the teacher an insight into the children's knowledge. We usually begin a theme by brainstorming for what the children know about a given subject. A lack of ideas indicates that the children may need a *refill* of language and knowledge. The brainstorming is continuously being added to as the theme is developed.

Brainstorming is a whole class activity. The teacher begins by asking a question such as "What is green?" and elicits responses from the children. As the children respond, the teacher draws the appropriate pictures on the chalkboard and the children chant. **Note:** at the beginning of the kindergarten year, draw a picture only. No words are needed.

After the brainstorming, again chant all the pictures that were drawn: "A leaf is green. A turtle is green. Grass is green. A car is green." As the year progresses you will want to add words to the brainstorming:

Most brainstorming needs to be saved! As you work through a theme you will be continually referring to these ideas. Copy the brainstorming onto cards or chart paper. The cards may be displayed using masking tape, sticky side out. The chart may be used for matching and rebuilding. At a later date the chart may be cut apart and made into a strip book.

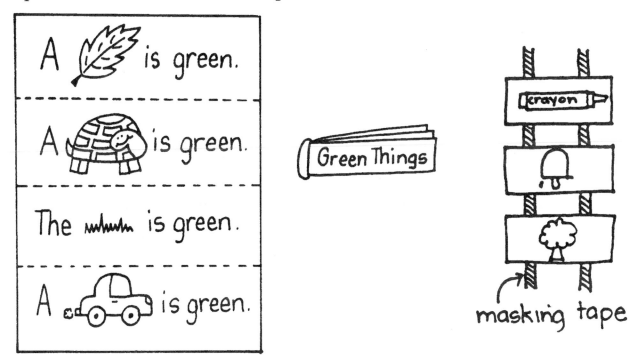

Another example of a brainstorming technique is to record ideas in categories that are not labeled. After the pattern is obvious, the children tell where to record the next idea. This method helps stimulate the children's thinking.

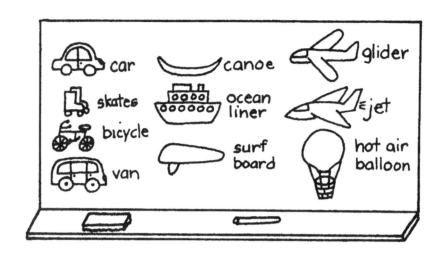

Sorting and Classifying:

 This when children look for likenesses and differences and put things together that are alike in some manner. The ideas from brain-storming activities are ideal for sorting and classifying. We usually begin classifying with groups of four to six children, with each group having about twenty cards or items to sort.

After this small group sorting activity, the whole class re-groups and chants. Example: We classified according to color and then chanted, "A chair is green. An olive is green. A fat frog is green, etc." Gradually, we work toward activities that will involve individual classifications. The results of these activities may be graphed, producing either a real graph or a pictorial graph.[1]

Develop in the Pocket Chart:

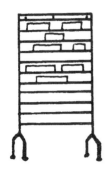

We use a pocket chart made of clear acetate and nylon.[2] You may use sentence strips or tagboard cards (laminated or contacted for a longer life) with the pocket chart. Whole texts, repeated phrases or pictures only may be used. There are a variety of ways to use the pocket chart. We listed our favorites:

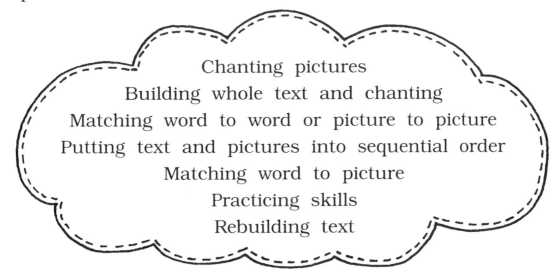

Chanting pictures
Building whole text and chanting
Matching word to word or picture to picture
Putting text and pictures into sequential order
Matching word to picture
Practicing skills
Rebuilding text

When we are developing a lesson in the pocket chart, we usually insert the appropriate pictures, or text and pictures, and then have the children chant **many** times. We may ask the children to hide their eyes and then we take something out of the text or merely turn it over.

The children then decide what is missing and chant to see if they are correct. We then take more than one word, picture, or phrase out (or turn them over) and repeat the process. The final task is to rebuild the entire text.

Samples:

Step 1:   Chanting pictures
           "A leaf is green."

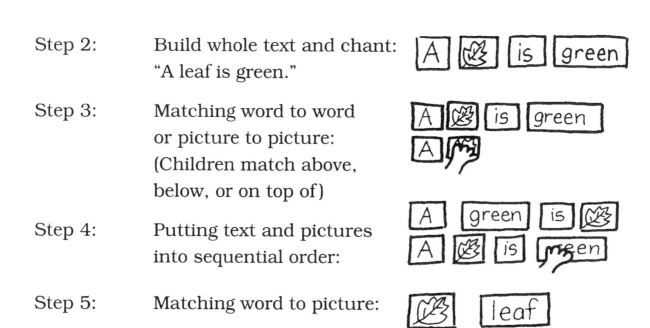

Step 2:   Build whole text and chant:
          "A leaf is green."

Step 3:   Matching word to word
          or picture to picture:
          (Children match above,
          below, or on top of)

Step 4:   Putting text and pictures
          into sequential order:

Step 5:   Matching word to picture:

Step 6:   Practicing skills:

- Find the word that says *green*.
- Find the word that says *is*.
- Find the word that comes before *green*.
- Find the word that comes after *is*.
- What sound do you hear at the
  beginning of the word *leaf*?

Step 7:   Rebuilding: all pictures and text are distributed to the
          children and the complete story is built again in the
          pocket chart. Children read the text from the pocket
          chart, checking for accuracy.

Tracking:

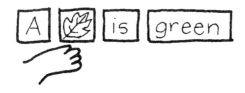

This involves moving your hand under
and pointing to each word as it is read.
This helps develop left to right pro-
gression as well as one-to-one correspondence between the printed text
and the spoken word.

Big Books:

These are enlarged versions of books, poems or songs. The print must be large enough so that it may be seen by the entire class. The enlarged print allows us to track as we read and helps to develop one-to-one correspondence. Many of the activities used with the pocket chart may also be used with big books. We laminate the pages of teacher-prepared big books and bind them with loose leaf rings. The rings may be taken out and the pages shuffled so that the children may sequence the big book. For obvious reasons **do not** number the pages. These books are really loved and used over and over by the children.

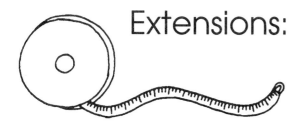

Extensions:

These are activities we practice what we learned during brain-storming, reading, chanting, and the various pocket chart activities. We try to incorporate the following:

Individual booklets – Each child makes his/her own booklet and should have the opportunity to read and track before taking it home.

Class book – Each child contributes a page and the book is kept in the classroom library.

Drama – Children act out the activity with **all** children taking **all** the parts. (a bit noisy but very effective)

Art – Children make illustrations for bulletin boards, booklets, plays, etc., using as many different kinds of art media as possible.

Make-a-play – Children retell a story by manipulating characters they have made.

Writing – All writing activities need to be extensively developed orally **first.**

1. Using a structure or frame, the children fill in the blanks by taking the ideas from the brainstorming activities.

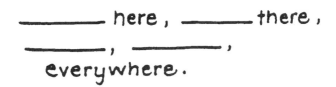

2. Creating innovations: children orally rewrite a familiar text using their own words. Example: (change "Brown bear, brown bear, what do you see?" to "Octopus, Octopus, what do you see?") This can be an individual or a whole group activity. The teacher may need to take dictation for the very young child.

3. Dictation: children individually illustrate and the teacher transcribes for them.

Draw with me – This is a whole class activity where language development is the goal. We do not consider this an art lesson. All the children are working with individual chalkboards at this time. We ask the children to name all the parts that need to be included to draw a specific object. A sample might be:

"What do we need to make a house?"

"A door"

"A roof"

"Windows"

(continue until entire picture is completed)

Individual sequencing – This is when each child puts pictures or a text into a specific order. This is usually a *cut and paste* activity. It varies in difficulty. We begin with pictures only, then pictures with the text, and finally the text alone. We also put the text in sequence with numerals, words, and pictures.

Pictures only:

Pictures with text:

Numeral, text and picture:

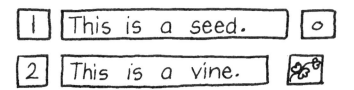

Homework – This is when we try to involve the family. The homework is occasional and we include a detailed explanation. This activity is returned to class and used for chanting, classifying booklet making or other language activities.

An example might be:

Dear Parents,

Our language arts theme this month is centered around plants. This week we are learning about seeds. Your child needs to bring a picture of something that grows from a seed. You may help your child draw or find a picture in a magazine. Please return the picture tomorrow.

Thank you for helping!

A follow-up activity might include sorting and classifying these pictures according to whether the plant produces food or not, i.e., flower, grapes, oak tree, oranges, etc. A booklet can then be made including all the homework pictures or individual booklets may be made from each classification.

1.Baratta-Lorton, Mary. **Mathematics Their Way**, Addison-Wesley Publishing Company, Reading, MA.
2. Available through *Teaching Resource Center*, P.O. Box 1509, San Leandro, CA 94577.

Introduction

This theme is written in a specific sequence, but it is merely a suggestion. You need not follow this exact order. Choose those activities that best suit your classroom. We have tried to select our materials carefully as many of you may not deal with the religious aspect of Christmas.

As we are developing our themes, we gather materials wherever we can find them. Obtaining the materials is quite easy (and fun!); the difficulty lies in narrowing the selections so that we include a variety of teaching strategies. We feel it is important to select a book for its strength and for the manner in which it can enrich the theme.

At the time this book went to press, all the books we have developed were in print. However, books are going in and out of print all the time. If you cannot locate a particular book, try the public library, your school library or contact a local bookstore and they might be able to track the selection down for you.

We hope you enjoy our selections and we are quite sure that you will add many of your own favorites. Merry Christmas!

Activity 1

It's Almost Christmas Time

 Materials:

- Blackline 1 for pocket chart song
- Blacklines 1–5 for noun wordbank
- Sentence strips
- Felt pens
- Stickers, five different designs per child
- 6″ x 9″ construction paper for sticker book, six per child
- Laminating film or contact paper
- Three pieces of 4½″ x 6″ red and green construction paper for the pocket chart.
- Strips of lined writing paper for first grade

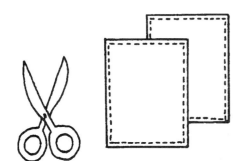 Preparation:

1. Duplicate three copies of each picture found on blackline 1 for the pocket chart song. Color, cut apart and laminate or contact. Add the red and green construction paper for the first verse. (**Note:** blackline 1 will be used two times.)

2. Color blacklines 1–5 for the noun wordbank. Cut apart, contact or laminate. Using sentence strips print matching word cards to correspond to the wordbank pictures.

3. Copy the following song on sentence strips and cut into individual word cards:

It's Almost Christmas Time

Red and green, everywhere
Red and green, everywhere
Red and green, everywhere
It's almost Christmas time!

Wreaths of holly on the door
Wreaths of holly on the door
Wreaths of holly on the door
It's almost Christmas time!

Christmas cookies on a plate
Christmas cookies on a plate
Christmas cookies on a plate
It's almost Christmas time!

Decorations on the tree
Decorations on the tree
Decorations on the tree
It's almost Christmas time

Stockings hung, all in a row
Stockings hung, all in a row
Stockings hung, all in a row
It's almost Christmas time!

4. **Sticker booklets:** each booklet consists of a cover and five pages of 6″ x 9″ construction paper. Depending upon the stickers you are able to find, prepare five sentence strips in the following manner and add the corresponding stickers:

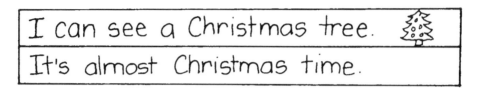

I can see a Christmas tree.

It's almost Christmas time.

I can see a snowman.

It's almost Christmas time.

I can see a wreath.

It's almost Christmas time.

I can see an angel.

It's almost Christmas time.

I can see Santa Claus.

It's almost Christmas time.

For **kindergarten** you will need to make your own blackline master of the sentence strips you prepared. (Each child needs one set of sentences.) When making the booklets, the children will cut these sentence strips apart. Using the pocket chart as a reference, the children will then match the sentences to the corresponding stickers.

For **first grade** either duplicate writing lines at the bottom of the 6" x 9" construction paper or cut writing paper into strips that may be pasted on the construction paper. The children will copy from the board or create their own sentences.

| I can see a Christmas tree. |
| It's almost Christmas time. |
| I can see a snowman. |
| It's almost Christmas time. |
| I can see a wreath. |
| It's almost Christmas time. |
| I can see an angel. |
| It's almost Christmas time. |
| I can see Santa Claus. |
| It's almost Christmas time. |

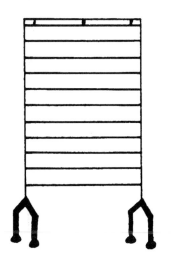

Procedure:

1. Introduce the song *It's Almost Christmas Time* in the pocket chart, using pictures only. (Sing this song to the tune of *Skip To My Lou*.)
2. Sing several times until the children know the tune and words.

3. Add the words, one line at a time, using phonetic clues until the entire text is built. Because of the repetition, this is an easy activity with which to begin this theme.

4. Distribute all word and picture cards and have the children rebuild the song as the class sings.

5. Brainstorm for other things that remind us of Christmas and begin a Christmas noun word-bank (We suggest transferring these ideas to picture and word cards and displaying them so children may not only see them but may easily manipulate them. Some teachers like to place these cards on the chalk tray while others like to place them in a pocket chart or on the bulletin board.).

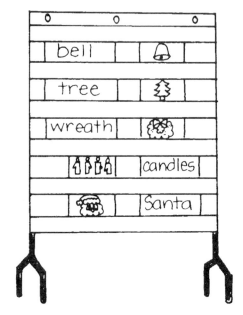

We have included some picture cards in the blackline masters to help you begin this wordbank. Other great sources are color books.

6. Use this wordbank daily. Some suggested activities are:
   Chant: using any simple frame sentence
   (I can see a _____, This is a _____, Here is a _____, etc.)
   Find your partner: distribute all word and picture cards. The children find the card that matches the one they have and return the pair to the pocket chart.
   Detective: before the children arrive, turn several picture cards over. The children solve the case of the missing pictures by either reading the words or using phonetic clues to help them unlock the words.

7. Using the ideas from the wordbank, the children are now able to create new verses for *It's Almost Christmas Time.*

Reindeer prancing through the snow
Reindeer prancing through the snow
Reindeer prancing through the snow
It's almost Christmas time.

Santa coming down the chimney

Bells are ringing everywhere...

Extension:

Christmas Sticker Booklet

Display the following in the pocket chart, using the prepared sentence strips and corresponding stickers. (**Note:** your sentences will depend on the stickers you are able to locate.)

Chant, calling attention to how the word **a** changes to **an** and why. Distribute the booklet pages and stickers. Kindergarten children will need a copy of the sentences that you prepared. First grade will need strips of lined writing paper. The children refer to the pocket chart and match each sentence and sticker, pasting one sticker and the appropriate sentence strip to each page. First grade students need to copy the sentences from the pocket chart and then add the corresponding sticker to each page. Staple, read together and take home.

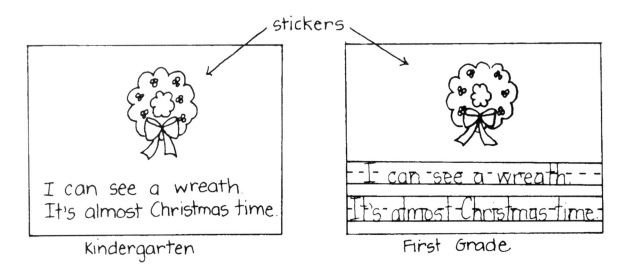

stickers

I can see a wreath.
It's almost Christmas time.

Kindergarten

I can see a wreath.
It's almost Christmas time.

First Grade

Note: sentences will vary according to stickers that you are able to find. If you wish, the children may illustrate in place of using stickers.

Activity 2 — *What Shall We Put On The Christmas Tree?*

Materials:

- Blacklines 6–16 for the big book
- Blackline 17 for a class book
- Blacklines 18–19 for the pocket chart
- Sentence strips
- Felt pens
- Laminating film or contact paper
- *The Family Christmas Tree Book* by Tomie De Paola
- Loose leaf ring
- Glitter, paint, material scraps for class book

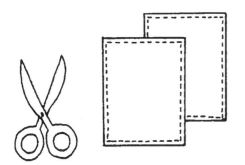

Preparation:

1. **Big Book:** color blacklines 6–16. Laminate or contact. Bind together with a loose leaf ring. (**Note:** If you would like to make a larger big book, enlarge each of the blacklines prior to coloring.)

2. **Pocket chart:** copy the text on to sentence strips and cut apart into word cards. The melody is found under Procedure and the text is found on Blacklines 6–16. Please note that you will have to have *three sets* of each repetitive phrase. Make three copies of blacklines 18–19 for the pocket chart. Color, cut apart and laminate or contact.

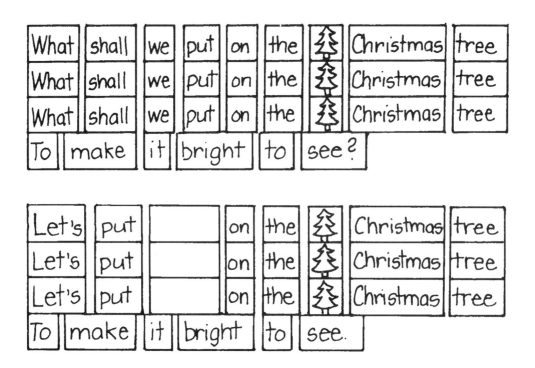

3. **Class book:** duplicate blackline 17, one per child, for the class book page. A cover might include a tree decorated with the ideas the children included in this book. Glitter adds a festive touch.

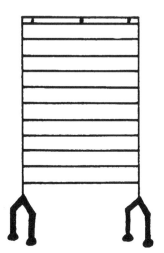

Procedure:

This is the music to the song *Christmas Tree* by Carolyn Meyer.
Note: when you are singing this song with the big book, sing the
top phrase three times and then sing the bottom phrase once.
What shall we put on the Christmas tree **(sing three times)** and
to make it bright to see **(sing one time).**

11

1. Prior to this activity, read *The Family Christmas Tree Book* by Tomie De Paola. (This may take more than one sitting as it contains quite a bit of information.) This will help give the children some general facts about trees and their decorations.

2. Introduce the song *Christmas Tree?* using the big book.

3. Sing several times, having the children join in as the teacher tracks the words. (Track the top phrase three times and track the bottom phrase once.) Sing until the children know the melody.

4. Place the words **What shall we put on the Christmas tree** in the first line of the pocket chart. Place the remaining words to the song at the bottom of the pocket chart in random order. The children may develop the next two lines by matching word to word with the first line. Help the children build the last line ("To make it bright to see?") using phonetic clues.

5. Build the remainder of the song, in the same manner, developing one line at a time.

6. Depending on the level of your class, you may wish to distribute all word and picture cards and have the children rebuild the song.

7. Brainstorm for other ideas to put on the Christmas tree. Record these on word and picture cards. Now insert these new ideas into the song. (In the interest of your sanity, may we offer a suggestion?) When using the new ideas, put three different things in each verse:

> **Let's put a cookie on the Christmas tree,**
> **Let's put popcorn on the Christmas tree,**
> **Let's put a snowman on the Christmas tree,**
> **To make it bright to see.**

Extension: *Class Book*

1. Chant the brainstormed ideas using the following frame:

> Our Christmas tree has _____.

2. Using a copy of blackline 17, each child chooses an idea and completes the frame. (Dictation may be necessary for Kindergarten.) Use felt pens, crayons, glitter, paint, old material scraps, yarn, etc. to illustrate. Bind pages together, read and add to your class library.

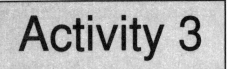 **Activity 3** *Christmas Trees*

 Materials:

- *A Christmas Promise* by Lark Carrier
- *Celebrations* by Marlene J. and Robert A. McCracken
- *Ed Emberley's Big Red Drawing Book* by Ed Emberley
- Sample branches from Christmas trees sold in your area
- 8–10 sentence strips for a strip book
- Rubber band for the strip book
- Individual chalkboards, erasers, chalk
- Large art paper, one per child, for extension picture
- Paint, colored pencils, pastels, crayons, felt pens, chalk or whatever you choose to use for the extension

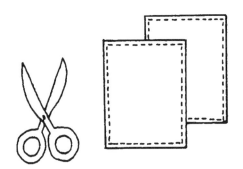 Preparation:

1. Schedule a field trip to a local Christmas tree lot. If this is not possible, invite the proprietor to bring many different samples of evergreen branches to your classroom. Try to include fir, spruce and pine.
2. Fold the sentence strips in half and bind with a rubber band for the strip book. Print "Christmas trees..." on the front.

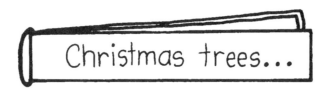

Christmas trees...

3. Select the art media you will use for the extension activity and have it available.

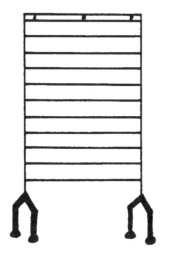

Procedure:

1. Read and enjoy *A Christmas Promise.* What kind of tree do you think this might be? What do you know about Christmas trees?

2. At this point brainstorm for all the things the children know about real evergreen trees. (**Note:** a wonderful background selection describing evergreen trees is found in *Celebrations* pages 43–45.)

3. Record this brainstorming on a large sheet of butcher paper. On the left side write, "Things we know." On the right side write, "Things we want to know."

Things We Know	Things We Want to Know
-trees are green	- What are pine cones for?
-trees are pretty	
-trees come in sizes	- What kinds of trees are used for Christmas trees?
-trees have pine cones	
-trees smell good	- How many . . .

4. Go on a field trip to a Christmas tree lot or invite the proprietor to your classroom for first hand information about evergreen trees. Be sure to have a sample of each type available for touch, smell and observation.

5. After the field trip or the presentation, refer to the butcher paper brainstorming. Make corrections and additions. Use the frame, "Christmas trees _____" and chant all the brainstormed facts.

6. Now record one fact on each page of the prepared strip book. (**Note:** folding eight to ten sentence strips will give you sixteen to twenty pages.)

7. Have the class read this *instant book* and add it to your classroom library.

1. Distribute chalkboards, chalk and erasers to each child. (Newsprint and pencil or black construction paper and chalk will work if you do not have individual chalkboards available.)

2. Ask the class, "What do Christmas trees have?" The teacher uses a large chalkboard and the children use individual chalkboards. As each attribute is mentioned, the teacher illustrates and the children copy. Continue with the process until the tree is completed. A great resource book for drawing is *Ed Emberley's Big Red Drawing Book*.

"What do Christmas trees have?"

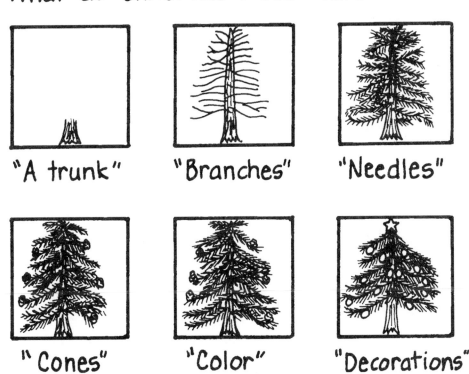

"A trunk"   "Branches"   "Needles"

"Cones"   "Color"   "Decorations"

3. Distribute art paper and what ever media you have chosen for your children. Using what they learned in the above lesson, the children now create their own pictures of Christmas trees.

Activity 4

I Like Trees

Materials:

- A copy of *Bugs* by Margaret Wise Brown
  (In *Hats, Pockets and Shoes,* published by Teaching Resource
  Center, P.O. Box 1509, San Leandro, CA 94577)
- Chart paper
- *The Cobweb Christmas* by Shirley Climo
- Blackline 20 of a tree shape for *Bugs* rewrite
- Blackline 21 for the kindergarten class book
- Lined writing paper
- Sentence strips
- Green construction paper for a tree shape
- Red hots (candy)
- Glow in the dark paint
- Q-tips

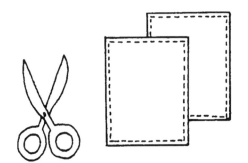

Preparation:

1. Copy the original poem, *Bugs*, onto large chart paper.
2. For first grade, duplicate blackline 20 of the tree shape on green construction paper, one per child.
3. For Kindergarten, copy blackline 21, one per child, for a class book.
4. Prepare sentence strips for a rewrite in the following manner:

| I like Christmas trees. |
| Any kind of Christmas trees. |
| _____ trees, |
| _____ trees, |
| _____ trees, |
| _____ trees, |
| Any kind of Christmas trees, |
| I like Christmas trees. |

| A tree _____, |
| A tree _____, |
| A tree _____, |
| A tree _____, |
| I like Christmas trees. |

(**Note:** we have given you a shortened version of the original poem. We feel it works better for younger children.)

Procedure:

1. Read and enjoy *The Cobweb Christmas*. Talk about the magical parts of Christmas. Discuss what Tante did to prepare for Christmas. What do you do to prepare for the holidays? Does your family have any special traditions? Tante remembered all the animals except for one. Which one was that? There is a passage that describes how the spiders entered Tante's home (*creeping, crawling, sneaking softly,...*) This is a marvelous opportunity for drama using their fingers for the spider movements.)

2. If your children are not familiar with the structure of the poem *Bugs*, display the poem and read or chant several times.

3. To prepare for an innovation on this structure, first brainstorm for words that describe Christmas trees (colors, kinds, sizes, etc.). Record this brainstorming on word cards.

4. Chant this brainstorming (lighted trees, shining trees, pine trees, tall trees, live trees, etc.).

5. Brainstorm for places you might see Christmas trees (in my window, on Gramma's table, in the forest, around the corner, behind the sofa, next to the fireplace, etc.). Record this brainstorming on word cards also.

6. Chant this brainstorming.

7. Place the sentence strips (structure) in the pocket chart. Display the wordcards from the brainstorming in another pocket chart, on a chalk tray or any other place where they are accessible to the children. (See illustration on page 19.)

8. Children may now create an innovation by placing the various brainstormed ideas into the structure and chanting. Although there is a rhyme in the second part of the structure, it is not necessary for children to reproduce a rhyming set. It will sound equally nice without the rhyme. A poem our children created is as follows:

I like Christmas trees.
Any kind of Christmas trees.
Green trees,
White trees,
Lighted trees,
Bright trees,
I like Christmas trees.

A tree in my window,
A tree down the hall,
A tree by the fireplace,
A tree at the mall,
I like Christmas trees.

9. Transfer this class innovation onto large chart paper, cut it into the shape of a Christmas tree and display.

Extensions: *Class Book and Rewrites*

Kindergarten class book: each child needs one copy of blackline 21 and chooses two adjectives to describe Christmas trees. The teacher or the child writes the words in the appropriate spaces. Children illustrate to match the adjectives. The pages are then compiled into a class book. A title might be "I Like Christmas Trees."

First grade rewrites: staple a piece of lined writing paper behind the green tree shape (blackline 20). We suggest stapling in each of the four corners. The children cut the tree shape and will end up with writing paper the same size. Using the structure in the pocket chart and the brainstormed ideas, the children can rewrite their own innovation on the tree-shaped lined paper. Glue this writing to the back of the green construction paper tree. To decorate the green construction paper tree, dip a Q-tip into glow in the dark paint and dot the tree. **Note:** *don't tell the children that the paint glows in the dark!* Glue down red hots for additional ornaments. Hang as a mobile so that both sides may be seen. For an added surprise, turn off the lights and watch the children as they realize their trees are glowing! (Kindergarten children could use blackline 20 as an art project.)

Santa's Journey

Materials:

- *Must Be Santa* by H. Moore and B. Fredericks
- Blacklines 22–23 of *Must Be Santa* pictures to be used in the pocket chart
- Sentence strips
- Blackline 24 of Santa finger puppet and Sleigh
- Blue construction paper for individual booklets
- White construction paper for booklet cover.
- Cotton balls
- Felt pens
- Contact paper or laminating film
- Strips of lined writing paper for first grade booklet

Preparation:

1. Color, cut and laminate Blacklines 22–23 of the *Must Be Santa* pictures for the pocket chart.

2. Using sentence strips, copy the chorus *(Must be Santa, Must be Santa...)* and labels to correspond with the eight blackline pictures (beard that's white, special night...) You will need to find a copy of the song as copyright prevents us from giving you the words. We found the words on a Raffi record, in a Raffi songbook and in the Class-Size Book.

3. Duplicate Blackline 24 of the sleigh and Santa finger puppet, one per child, on white construction paper.

4. If you choose to use the Class-Size book, be sure to coordinate the coloring with the pocket chart pictures.

Procedure:

Note: prior to this lesson, teach the song *Must Be Santa.*

1. Introduce *Must Be Santa,* beginning with the Class-Size Book or by sequencing the pictures in the pocket chart.

2. Place the first line of the chorus in the pocket chart. Have the children read. Using this first line as a model, the children build the remainder of the chorus.

3. Sing the entire song, tracking the words of the chorus each time it is sung.

24

4. Sing again, sequencing the pictures in the pocket chart.
5. Using phonetic clues, the children match each phrase to the corresponding picture.

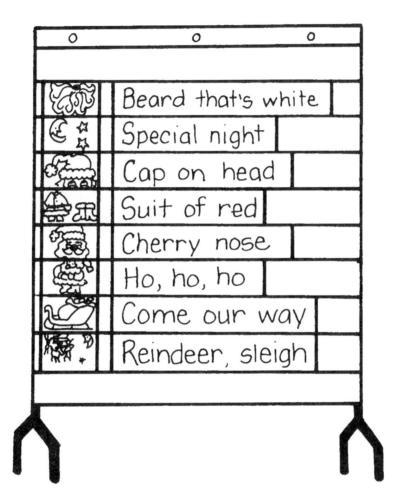

6. Sing again, tracking in the pocket chart.
7. Distribute all pictures and phrase cards. The children find their partners and rebuild this in the pocket chart.
8. Sing again and check for accuracy.
9. Santa takes a long journey on Christmas Eve. Brainstorm on the chalkboard for places that he might encounter on his way to our neighborhood. Be sure to elicit a prepositional phrase with each place that is mentioned.

...around the bike racks,
...through the golden arches at MacDonalds,
...over the San Joaquin River,
...under the power lines,
...past the mall,
...etc.

10. Decide whether you or the class will choose the places that Santa will go on this journey. For the extension you will need to duplicate sentence strips of the chosen prepositional phrases for kindergarten children. First grade children may copy the phrases from the chalkboard on to lined strips of paper.

Extension: *Santa's Journey Booklet*

For the cover use blue 9″ x 12″ construction paper. Cut white construction paper for the snow. You may wish to add salt to white paint and lightly go over the snow area. This creates a wonderful texture. Using blackline 24, color and cut the sleigh and Santa finger puppet. Glue the sleigh along the sides and bottom, being careful to leave room for the puppet to easily ride in the sleigh. Glue the puppet tabs together and place Santa in the sleigh.

The art work for the remainder of the of the pages will depend on the brainstormed prepositional phrases that were chosen in your classroom. We like to end this book with "and got home in time for dinner." Here is a copy of one of the brainstormed booklets from our class:

Cover

Santa Claus went on a journey

around the bike racks at Creekside,

down the slide at Laughlin Park,

through the golden arches,

past the skaters at Hammer Skate,

through the fast lane at Fry's,

up through the fog,

and got home in time for dinner!

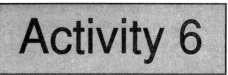

Activity 6

Bah! Humbug?

Materials:

- *Fat Santa* by Margery Cuyler
- *Bah! Humbug?* by Lorna Balian
- Lightweight string
- Scrap paper, yarn, staples, glue, felt pens, material scraps and any other items that you wish to use for a trap.
- Drawing paper
- Cat's Cradle reference books, if necessary (titles found under Extension activity)

Preparation:

1. Cut string for each child to make a *Cat's Cradle.*

Procedure:

1. Read and enjoy *Fat Santa*. Discuss the trap in which Santa was caught. Was this trap an intentional one? Have you ever thought about trying to catch Santa?

2. Brainstorm orally for ways to trap Santa. Include any materials you would need and ways these materials would be used.
   (Be sure to spend an adequate amount of time developing these ideas as they will be used again the following day.)

3. The following day:
   Kindergarten: actually build a trap to catch Santa using a small area in your classroom. Be sure to have on hand the items the children listed on the previous day. This would be a great opportunity for drama! "Can you show me how Santa would look if he got caught in your trap?"

   Grade One: Each child needs a sheet of drawing paper to illustrate the method he/she would use to trap Santa. Have available scrap materials, paper, staples, etc. for the children to use in building their trap. Depending upon ability, children write a sentence or two and take turns sharing their ideas. These pages might later be bound together for a class book entitled *The Trap*.

4. Read *Bah! Humbug?*. Compare this trap with the traps that were constructed. How are they similar and different?

Extension: Cat's Cradle

Make a *Cat's Cradle.* There are two books that clearly illustrate the first stages of this string game and are helpful if you do not know how to make a Cat's Cradle. The two books are:

Helfman, Harry & Elizabeth, *Strings on Your Fingers,* William Morrow & Co., New York, 1965.

Gryski, Camilla, *Cat's Cradle, Owls Eyes: A Book Of String Games,* William Morrow & Co., New York, 1984.

Activity 7 *Santa Mouse*

Materials:

- *Santa Mouse* by Michael Brown
- Blacklines 22–23 of *Must Be Santa* pictures (from Activity 5)
- Individual chalkboards, chalk and erasers
- Blackline 25 for build-up book (first grade)
- Blackline 26 for build-up book (kindergarten)
- Blackline 27 for star Santa (cover for booklet)
- 9″ x 12″ red construction paper for the star Santa
- 9″ x 12″ green construction paper, two per child, for booklet cover
- 2½″ square of pink construction paper, one per child
- Cotton balls or cotton batting
- Large chart paper (optional)

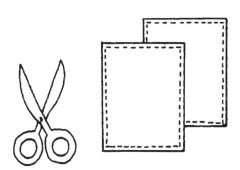

Preparation:

1. If you did not prepare this before, color, cut and laminate blacklines 22–23 of *Must Be Santa.*
2. For first grade, duplicate blackline 25. Staple so that each child has a booklet with seven pages.

3. For kindergarten, make six copies of blackline 26. The teacher needs to print six selected brainstormed sentences **before** duplicating the copies for the children. (See complete description and illustrations under Extension.) After you have prepared the six blacklines, duplicate so that each child has a stapled set of all six pages.

4. Using red construction paper, duplicate blackline 27, one per child. This star will be used to make a Santa for the cover.

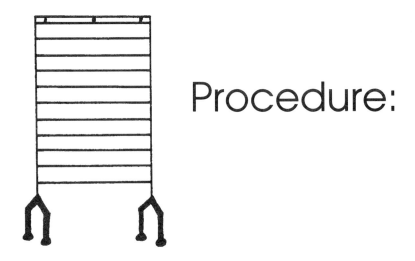

Procedure:

1. Read and enjoy the book, *Santa Mouse.*

2. Brainstorm, illustrating on the chalkboard as you go, for all the items Santa gave the little mouse so he would look like Santa. (boots, beard, belt, hat, suit)

3. What other things might Santa have that the mouse did not have? Add to the illustrated brainstorming. (A bag of toys, reindeer, sleigh, house at the North Pole, cherry nose, elves, workshop, etc.) **Save this brainstorming for the extension activity.**

4. Sing *Must Be Santa,* using the pocket chart pictures. (Refer to Activity 5.) Add to the brainstorming if needed.

5. On the chalkboard write:

   This is Santa Claus.

   He has _____

   Using the above structure, chant each of the brainstormed items.

6. Distribute individual chalkboards to each child. Using the *draw with me* technique, draw Santa. Be sure to include all the brainstormed attributes in the drawings. *Ed Emberley's Big Red Drawing Book* contains simplified drawings of Santa that you might find helpful.

What does Santa have?

"A beard."
"A cherry nose."
"Boots."
"A belt."
etc.

Extension: *Santa Build-Up Booklet*

(The build-up book was created by Marlene and Robert McCracken and is described in detail on pages 8–9 in *The Halloween Theme Book*, written by Marlene and Robert McCracken, published by Peguis Publishers Limited, 462 Hargrave St., Winnipeg, MB R3A OX5, 1984.)

For Kindergarten:

1. On large chart paper or on the chalkboard, print the heading, **This is Santa.**
2. Referring back to the brainstorming, the class chooses five attributes that describe Santa. Record these attributes under the heading and have the class read.
3. To prepare the blacklines for the build-up booklet pages, complete the following steps:

page 1

A. Using a copy of blackline 26, print the heading **This is Santa** on the right half of the paper.

This is Santa.
He has black boots.

page 2

B. Using another copy of the same blackline, print the heading and the first attribute. (**Note:** the children will have a blank Santa on the left hand side of each page to color as shown in the illustration of page one. We have shown what the children will illustrate.)

This is Santa.
He has black boots
He has a white beard.
He has a red hat.

page 4

C. Continue in the same manner until about five attributes have been listed. The children color the picture on each page to correspond to the text. Coloring the pictures *builds up* as each page is added.

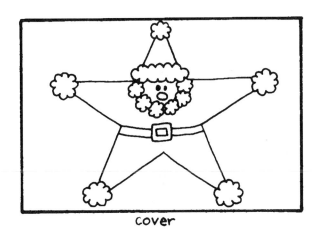

cover

D. For the cover, cut the red star shape (blackline 27) and mount on a piece of 9″ x 12″ green construction paper. Draw acircle shape on the 2½″ piece of pink construction paper. Add eyes and nose features with a crayon. Cut the circle and glue in place. Using a crayon, draw a black belt and then add cotton for the finishing touches. Using a blank piece of green paper for the back and the completed star Santa for the front, staple the covers onto the completed booklet.

For First Grade:

On large chart paper or on the chalkboard print the heading **This is Santa.** Referring back to the brainstorming, the class chooses six attributes that describe Santa. Record these attributes under the heading and have the class read. Distribute stapled copies of blackline 25 to the children. The class writes the sentences using the same format as explained in the build-up booklet for kindergarten. Add the star Santa cover.

page 3

Another option we like to offer children is to allow them the opportunity to choose their own attributes and make their booklets accordingly. They will still refer to the brainstorming for ideas but will have the freedom to expand and create their own individual Santas.

Activity 8 *Nicky's Christmas Surprise*

 Materials:

- *Nicky's Christmas Surprise* by Harriet Ziefert
- Blacklines 28–31 for the pocket chart
- Sentence strips
- Felt pens
- Contact paper or laminating film
- Selection of empty boxes
- *Boxes! Boxes!* by Leonard Everett Fisher
- Blacklines 32–33 of poem pictures for the pocket chart and sentence strips for the booklet.
- Each child needs seven pieces of 6" x 9" construction paper (any color you choose) to make the booklet for the extension
- 4" x 4" colored construction for the large gift—one per child
- 2" x 2" colored construction for the small gift—one per child
- 3" diameter colored construction for round gift—one per child
- 4" x 1½" colored construction for the tall gift—one per child
- Each child needs one red heart shape (blackline 33 has a pattern)
- Strips of lined writing paper for first grade extension
- Yarn or ribbon for each page of the booklet
- 8½" x 5½" wrapping paper for the cover of the booklet
- Optional: a small picture of each child
- Optional: a gift tag for the booklet cover
- *The Gift of the Magi* by O. Henry

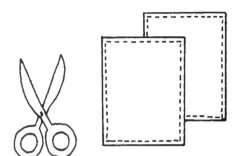

Preparation:

1. Color, cut, laminate or contact pictures from blacklines 28–31.

2. Using the book, *Nicky's Christmas Surprise*, as a guide, print the following on a sentence strip:

> "I'll visit the _____ ."

3. On a second sentence strip print the question Nicky asks each animal.

> I'll ask, "What sh. . .   ?"

4. Print each of the seven prepositional phrases on sentence strips.

> in his kennel.   etc.

5. Print the following poem, *Gifts* on sentence strips:

> **Gifts**
> **Some gifts are large,**
> **Some gifts are small,**
> **Some gifts are round,**
> **Some gifts are tall,**
> **But a gift from the heart**
> **Is the best gift of all!**

5. Color, cut and laminate or contact Blackline 32 and the heart at the top of Blackline 33. **Note:** The heart is for the pocket chart. You will need to trace it *(before you color it)* and make a copy for each child to use in the extension booklet.

6. For kindergarten: duplicate the sentence strips of the poem found on Blackline 33, one set per child.

Procedure:

1. Read and enjoy *Nicky's Christmas Surprise.* As you read the story, have the children predict what they think each animal will suggest for a gift.

2. Ask the children which animal Nicky went to see first. Place that picture in the pocket chart. Continue with each animal, using the book as a reference if needed. **Note:** leave the top two pockets empty. They will be used in step 5.

3. Display the gift pictures where they can be easily seen and obtained by the children. The children match each gift to the appropriate animal.

4. Remove the *gift* pictures from the pocket chart, leaving the *animal* pictures in place. Display the prepositional phrases where they can easily be seen and obtained. Using phonetic clues, help the children read the phrases. The children then add these to the pocket chart next to the appropriate animal pictures.

dog	in his kennel
bear	in his den
goat	in his shed
horse	in his barn
pig	in his sty
sheep	in their house
birds	in the yard

5. In the *top two pockets* of the pocket chart place the two sentence strips that were made in Steps two and three under *Preparation*. Help the children read the sentence strips.

6. Reread the story. Each time the two repeated lines:

I'll visit the _____

and

I'll ask, "What shall... ?"

appear, the appropriate animal picture and prepositional phrase are added to the pocket chart and the children read. Continue in this manner, changing each animal picture and prepositional phrase, until the entire book is developed.

7. If Nicky put all the gifts for his mom in boxes, what type boxes would he use? Can we guess what is in a box by its shape? What shape boxes have you seen? Have you ever been fooled by the shape?

8. Bring in a selection of empty boxes. Brainstorm for items that would fit in the different boxes. You might want to bring in pictures and the children can match a picture with a box.

9. Read *Boxes! Boxes!* and discuss the new boxes found in this book. (This story is full of rich vocabulary.)

10. Using blacklines 32–33 and sentence strips, introduce the poem *Gifts* in the pocket chart. Read and chant several times. The rhythm and rhyme makes this poem easily memorized.

11. Discuss with the class what a gift from the heart might be.

12. Depending on the maturity of your children, you may wish to read *The Gift of the Magi* by O. Henry. The version we like is published by Ideals Children's Books, Tennessee, 1989.

Extension: *Gifts Booklet*

The booklet is put together in the following manner:

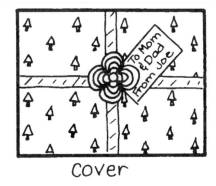

Cover

Some gifts are large,	Some gifts are small,
Some gifts are round,	Some gifts are tall,
But the gift from the heart is the best gift of all!	Merry Christmas school photo

Note: children may opt to draw the ribbons and bows with crayon or you may wish to have available yarn or ribbon. Stick-on bows are a nice added touch for the cover. We like to add a gift tag on the cover also.

We would like to thank the Lodi teacher that shared this poem and booklet with us during a workshop. We are sorry we do not have your name as we would like to acknowledge you for this wonderful idea.

42

Activity 9 — *The Twelve Days of Christmas*

 Materials:

- *The Twelve Days of Christmas* (One traditional copy and any other versions that are available to you)
- Blacklines 34–38 of *Twelve Days* pocket chart pictures, ordinal numerals (1st–12th) and cardinal numerals (2–12 and A)
- Large sheet of green butcher paper for bulletin board
- Sentence strips
- Painting paper, tempra paint
- Contact paper or laminating film
- Felt pens

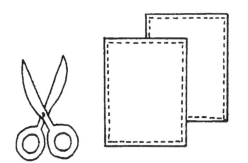

Preparation:

1. Color, cut and contact or laminate blacklines 34–38.
2. Cut a large Christmas tree shape from the green butcher paper. Make it as large as the bulletin board will allow.
3. Cut the bulletin board letters **Our 12 Days of Christmas** and display in the following manner:

Procedure:

1. Read any **traditional** version of *The Twelve Days of Christmas*. (The song, *The Twelve Days of Christmas*, refers to the period of time between Christmas and Epiphany, January 6)
2. Read again (or sing) with the children joining in during the count-down.

3. Teacher places all the ordinal numeral cards in the pocket chart. Chant with the class, "1st day, 2nd day, 3rd day, etc."
4. Distribute the cardinal numeral cards to the class. Have the children sequence these cards in the pocket chart along side the ordinal numerals.
5. Now distribute the picture cards to the class. Have the children add these to the pocket chart in the correct sequence.

6. Chant or sing from the pocket chart.
7. Distribute all picture and numeral cards and have the class rebuild. Sing to check for accuracy. At this point, read any other versions of this story that you can find. Compare the stories. Some of the books we like to use are *A Small Sheep In A Pear Tree* by Adrianne Lobel, *Snoopy and The 12 Days of Christmas* by Charles Schulz and *Twelve Cats for Christmas* by Martin Leman.

8. To prepare for a rewrite, ask the class if they know anyone who has received these kinds of gifts for Christmas. Using the chalkboard, brainstorm for kinds of gifts that they would like to receive:

9. One way to use this brainstorming is to create a bulletin board using a class rewrite. The class as a whole decides which twelve items to use in the new version. The children then assign a cardinal numeral to each gift. Now, chanting as you go, include additional words to maintain the meter of the original song. *(6 dollies napping, 5 fuzzy bears, 4 shiny bikes, ...)* See Extension for making the actual bulletin board.

10. Another way to use this brainstorming is for each child to create an individual version called *My Twelve Days of Christmas*. Before attempting this version, it is vital to begin with a great deal of oral work. We advise you, an aide or a parent volunteer to help the children with the meter by helping them choose the additional words. Make a note of the pattern used in the original song. It is not imperative for the children to have the exact format, but it sings better if you do.

This bulletin board is an illustration of the class rewrite called *Our 12 Days of Christmas.* Divide up the number of gifts (there are 78!) so that each child has two or three to make. We like to have the children use tempra and paint the items. We then add felt pen features or outlines, cut the pictures out and add them to the bulletin board tree. Write the words on sentence strips and place these below each item.

The Polar Express

Materials:

- *The Polar Express* by Chris Van Allsburg
- Small jingle bells, one per child
- Ribbon or yarn for the bells
- Pattern blocks
- White construction paper for snowflakes
- Blackline 39 of pattern block shapes
- Blackline 40 of jingle bell shape for class book
- Sentence strips for reindeer strip book
- Rubberband
- Dark blue construction paper, one per child, for mounting pattern block snowflakes

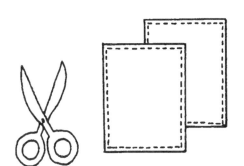

Preparation:

1. Duplicate blackline 39 on white construction paper, about three or four per child.

2. Duplicate blackline 40 on white construction paper, one per child, for the class book. Also duplicate one for the cover on any color of your choice. To make the covers, staple the jingle bell shape to a blank piece of construction paper of the same color, cut, and you will have a front and back cover that are the same size.

3. Tie each small jingle bell with a piece of ribbon or yarn long enough to encircle the child's wrist.

4. Prepare the strip book. Fold six to eight sentence strips. Bind in the middle with a rubber band.
(This will give you 12–16 pages) On the front write *Reindeer...*

cover

5. You may need to do a bit of research on reindeer. Below are some basic facts to add to your list.

- are native to northern Europe and Asia
- are related to the North American caribou
- can be tamed
- have large, deeply cleft hooves
- have hairy muzzles
- have antlers
- stand about 3½ feet high
- weigh 300 pounds
- can draw sleigh over snow 12–15 miles per hour
- can carry load up to 300 pounds
- feed on grass and lichens that grow in Arctic regions
- run in herds
- are Santa's favorite animals

Procedure:

1. Talk about the North Pole. Use a globe or map and help the children locate the North Pole.

2. Ask the children to tell you everything they know about reindeer. Read any factual books you have on reindeer. Discuss this information and review what the children initially came up with. Are there any facts that need to be altered or revised?

3. Now record one fact on each page of the prepared strip book. Have the class read this *instant book* and add it to your library.

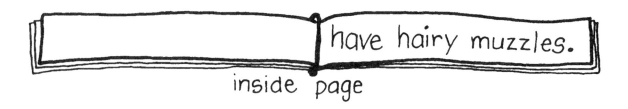

inside page

4. Tell the children that you have a wonderful story that involves something special from one of Santa's reindeer.

5. Hold up the book, *The Polar Express*, calling attention to the cover, front and back. Ask the children to tell you what they think this story will be about. Ask them what the words *Polar Express* mean. Discuss.

6. Read and enjoy the book, *The Polar Express*. **Stop** at the point

after the little boy reaches into his robe pocket and discovers the bell is gone. This is a nice opportunity for drama. Children can take turns describing what they think the little boy's reactions will be. The entire class then dramatizes each idea. Ask the children what they think happened to the bell. Now finish reading the story.

7. Discuss what hearing the bell means. Distribute the wrist jingle bells to the class and listen to them ask each other, "Can you hear the bell? I can hear the bell!"

Class book: if you were at the North Pole and Santa asked you

Extensions: *Class book and pattern block snowflakes*

what *one* thing you would like for Christmas, what would you choose? Encourage children to close their eyes and think carefully. Now distribute the bell shape from blackline 40 and ask the children to illustrate their gift. At the kindergarten level the teacher may wish to take dictation while a first grade child may write his/her own sentence. Bind these pages into a class book. A suggested title might be *The First Gift of Christmas*.

Pattern block snowflakes: refer to pages 9.6 to 9.7 in *Mathematics*

cover

inside page

Their Way Summary Newsletter by the Center for Innovation in Education. We suggest the children build symmetrical patterns with actual pattern blocks and then reproduce these patterns by gluing the white pattern block shapes that were cut from blackline 39 to a piece of dark blue construction paper. Display around the classroom.

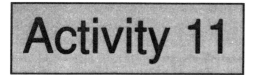

Activity 11

A Little House of Brown

Materials:

- Sentence strips
- 9" x 12" brown construction paper, two pieces, for big book covers
- Blackline 41 for big book cover
- Blackline 42–48 for the big book pages
- Sticky stars
- Yarn for hair
- Glitter
- Blacklines 49–50 for the pocket chart pictures
- Blackline 51 for ABC Christmas booklet page
- Felt pens
- Laminating film or contact paper
- Loose leaf rings

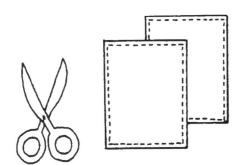

Preparation:

1. **Note:** if you plan to make an individual booklet of *A Little House of Brown*, reduce blacklines 41–48 *before* you make the big book!

2. **Big Book:** Color blacklines 41–48. *Cut the items from blackline 41 only.* (The pictures on this blackline will be glued to the front cover.) Add sticky stars to the tree (blackline 42) and sprinkle glitter on the bulbs (blackline 43). You will need to color and laminate blackline 44 *before* you glue yarn hair on the children.

3. Using brown construction paper, make the front cover in the following manner:

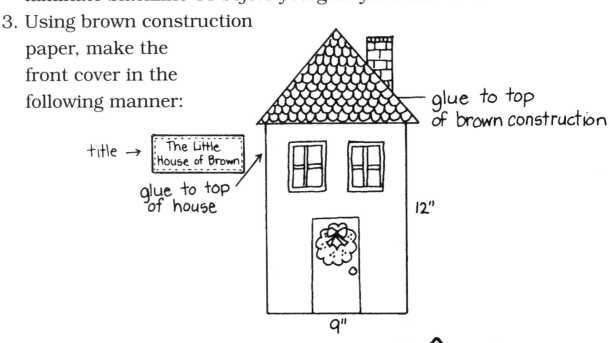

title →

The Little House of Brown

glue to top of house

glue to top of brown construction

12"

9"

4. To prepare the remaining pages of this book, copy the text on white paper and glue each verse on the back of the opposite page:

One cold ~

54

5. The text is as follows:

page 1   One cold Monday morning
On my way to town,
I saw 1 tree shining
In a little house of brown.

page 2   One cold Tuesday morning
On my way to town,
I saw 2 bulbs glittering
In a little house of brown.

page 3   One cold Wednesday morning
On my way to town,
I saw 3 children singing
In a little house of brown.

page 4   One cold Thursday morning
On my way to town,
I saw 4 stockings hanging
In a little house of brown.

page 5   One cold Friday morning
On my way to town,
I saw 5 bells ringing
In a little house of brown.

page 6   One cold Saturday morning
On my way to town,
I saw 6 cookies baking
In a little house of brown.

page 7   One cold Sunday morning
On my way to town,
I saw 7 candles glowing
In a little house of brown.

This general counting sequence idea was shared with us by Marlene and Robert McCracken in one of their workshops. We like to include countdowns in all our themes.

6. Contact or laminate each of the pages of the big book and bind together with loose leaf rings.

7. Color, cut and laminate the pocket chart pictures from blacklines 49–50. You may wish to add sticky stars and glitter before you laminate.

8. Print the following frame on sentence strips:

> **One cold** _____ **morning**
> **On my way to town,**
> **I saw** ____ _____ _____
> **In a little house of brown.**

9. Print the following words on sentence strips and cut apart into individual word cards:

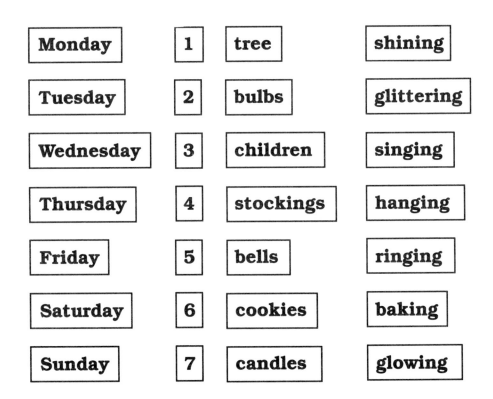

Monday	1	tree	shining
Tuesday	2	bulbs	glittering
Wednesday	3	children	singing
Thursday	4	stockings	hanging
Friday	5	bells	ringing
Saturday	6	cookies	baking
Sunday	7	candles	glowing

10. Duplicate blackline 51, one per child, for the ABC Christmas Book.

Procedure:

1. Teach the song, *Sing A Song For Christmas.*

2. Brainstorm for other things we do at Christmas time.
   (Trim the tree for Christmas, ring a bell for Christmas, wrap a gift for Christmas, bake some cookies for Christmas, etc.) The class sings and dramatizes as each new idea is brainstormed.

3. This song could easily be developed in the pocket chart and made into a class book. If you have the luxury of extra time, we suggest you consider these two options.

4. Before introducing *A Little House of Brown,* you may wish to review the names of the days of the week.

57

5. Using the big book you made, read the countdown, *A Little House of Brown.*

6. Read the book again, using the my turn, your turn technique. (The children will have no difficulty because of the many repetitions.)

7. Sequence the names of the days of the week in the pocket chart.

8. Distribute numeral cards and the pocket chart pictures to the class. The children add the appropriate pictures and numeral cards, one at a time, to the pocket chart. Check for accuracy by chanting or by rereading the big book.

9. If you have two pocket charts, leave the above in place. If you do not, remove the cards and display them on the chalkboard tray or any other place that is easily accessible to the children. Place the following frame in the pocket chart:

> One cold _____ morning
> On my way to town,
> I saw ___ _____ _____
> In a little house of brown.

10. With the help of the children, build the Monday verse in the pocket chart. (Add the words *Monday, 1, tree, shining* and the pocket chart picture of the tree.) Read together.

11. Continue in the same manner, placing the new word cards on top of the previous verse until the entire book has been developed.

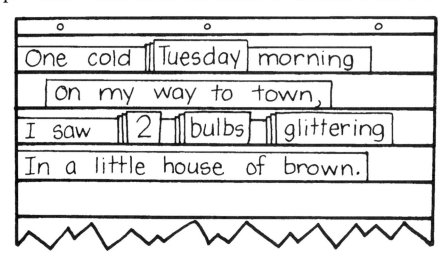

12. Reread from the big book.

ABC Christmas Book: On the chalkboard write the twenty-six letters of the alphabet. Ask the children to think of some Christmas things that begin with each letter. As the children mention an item, record it on the chalkboard and illustrate with a small picture:

To make this class book, each child selects one letter of the alphabet and completes blackline 51 with an illustration and the necessary words. For kindergarten the teacher may wish to take dictation while a first grade child may write the words. If you have more than twenty six children in your class, a title page, a cover (front and back), an author's signature page, etc. may be completed by the remaining children. Bind the pages together, read and add to your class library.

Additional Ideas: An individual booklet of *A Little House Of Brown* may be made by reducing blacklines 41–48 and duplicating the words of the counting structure.

The countdown may be rewritten by the class as a whole or by individual children. Brainstorm for things that can be seen at Christmas time and encourage the children to design the pages. The frame may be duplicated so the children add the missing words or, if the children are able, write the entire verse.

Optional Activities

Listed below are a few additional activities that may easily be incorporated into a Christmas theme. The descriptions are brief but we are sure you will find many creative ways to extend them.

Brown Bear, Brown Bear, What Do You See?: This is a natural for a rewrite. Read the book until the pattern is established and brainstorm for Christmas symbols. You may wish to begin with, "Yellow Star, Yellow Star, What do you see?" and end with "I See Santa Looking At Me." This may be made into a large class book or into small individual booklets. You may write the book together as a class, or have the children create their own versions.

The Gingerbread Man: You will need any version of the book. Read several times and dramatize. There are several opportunities for extensions with this book. A bulletin board may be made with each child using a gingerbread shape and decorating it with wallpaper, old material, ric-rac, ribbon, yarn, buttons, etc. Arrange the gingerbread men on the bulletin board so they are randomly running. Add the words, "Run, run, as fast as you can. You can't catch me, I'm the gingerbread man!" Another fun activity is to bake individual gingerbread men or to make one large class gingerbread man. Have the cookies *run away* and enjoy the chase. Be sure to enlist the help of your staff!

The Night Before Christmas: Read any version of this book to the children. Be sure to talk about the descriptive words found in this selection. After dramatizing it, you may wish to work with rhyme. Another idea is to have the children close their eyes and imagine what their *vision of sugar plums* would be. A class book could be made with these ideas.

Cooking: Reindeer sandwiches are lots of fun. Spread peanut butter on wheat bread and fold it over into a triangle. Add pretzels for the antlers, raisins for eyes, and a cherry for his nose. This activity could be incorporated with *Rudolph The Red Nosed Reindeer.*

Bibliography

Although we have made every effort to locate the current copyright holders of the materials used in this theme book, some we were unable to trace. We will be happy to correct any errors or omissions.

Balian, Lorna, *Bah! Humbug?*, Abingdon Press, Nashville, TN, 1987.

Brown, Marc, *Arthur's Christmas*, Little, Brown and Company, Boston, MA, 1984.

Brown, Margaret Wise, *The Little Fir Tree*, Harper & Row Publishers, New York, NY, 1985.

Brown, Michael, *Santa Mouse*, Grosset & Dunlap, New York, NY, 1981.

Carrier, Lark, *A Christmas Promise*, Picture Book Studio Ltd., Matick, MA, 1986.

Center for Innovation in Education, *Mathematics Their Way Summary Newsletter*, Saratoga, CA, 1988

Climo, Shirley, *The Cobweb Christmas*, Thomas Y. Crowell, New York, NY, 1982.

Cuyler, Margery, *Fat Santa*, Henry Holt and Company, New York, NY, 1987.

De Paola, Tomie, *The Family Christmas Tree Book*, Holiday House, New York, NY, 1980.

Emberley, Ed, *Ed Emberley's Bid Red Drawing Book*, Little, Brown and Company, Boston, MA, 1987.

Fisher, Leonard Everett, *Boxes! Boxes!*, The Viking Press, New York, NY, 1984.

Gackenbach, Dick, *Claude The Dog, A Christmas Story*, Clarion Books, New York, NY, 1974.

Gammell, Stephen, *Wake Up, Bear...It's Christmas!*, Lothrop, Lee & Shepard Books, New York, NY, 1981.

Gryski, Camilla, *Cat's Cradle, Owls Eyes; A Book Of String Games*, William Morrow & Co., New York, NY, 1984.

Haber, Jon Z., *Deck The Halls*, Grosset & Dunlap, New York, NY, 1989.

Helfman, Harry & Elizabeth, *Strings On Your Fingers*, William Morrow & Co., New York, NY, 1984.

Henry, O., *The Gift of the Magi*, Ideals Publishing Corporation, Nashville, TN, 1989.

Knight, Hilary, *The Twelve Days of Christmas*, Macmillan Publishing Co., Inc., New York, NY, 1981.

Leman, Martin, *Twelve Cats For Christmas*, Pelham Books, London, England, 1982.

Lobel, Adrianne, *A Small Sheep In A Pear Tree*, Harper & Row, New York, NY, 1977.

Marshall, James, *Merry Christmas, Space Case*, Dial Books for Young Readers, New York, NY, 1989.

McCracken, Marlene J. and Robert A., *Celebrations*, Peguis Publishers Limited, Winnipeg, Canada, 1986.

McCracken, Marlene J. and Robert A., *Halloween*, Peguis Publishers Limited, Canada, 1984.

McCracken, Marlene J. and Robert A., *Toys*, Peguis Publishers Limited, Winnipeg, Canada, 1989.

Moore, H. and Fredericks, B., *Must Be Santa*, Published by Class-Size Books, P.O. Box 366, Port Coquitlam, B.C., Canada, V3C 4K6

Pearson, Tracey Campbell, *We Wish You A Merry Christmas*, Dial Books for Young Readers, New York, 1983.

Reece, Colleen L., *My First Christmas Book*, Childrens Press, Chicago, IL, 1984.

Schulz, Charles M., *Snoopy and the Twelve Days Of Christmas Pop-Up Book*, Determined Productions, Inc., San Francisco, CA, 1984.

Windham, Sophie, *Twelve Days of Christmas*, G. P. Putnam's Sons, New York, NY, 1986.

Ziefert, Harriet, *Nicky's Christmas Surprise*, Puffiln Books, Viking Penguin Inc., New York, NY, 1985.

Blacklines

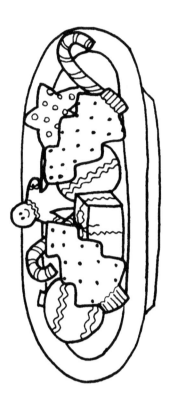

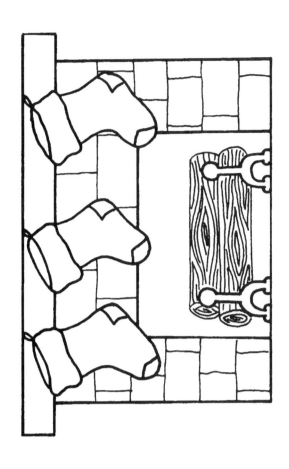

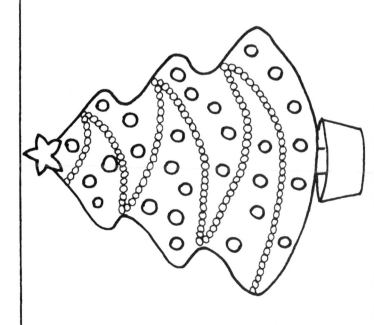

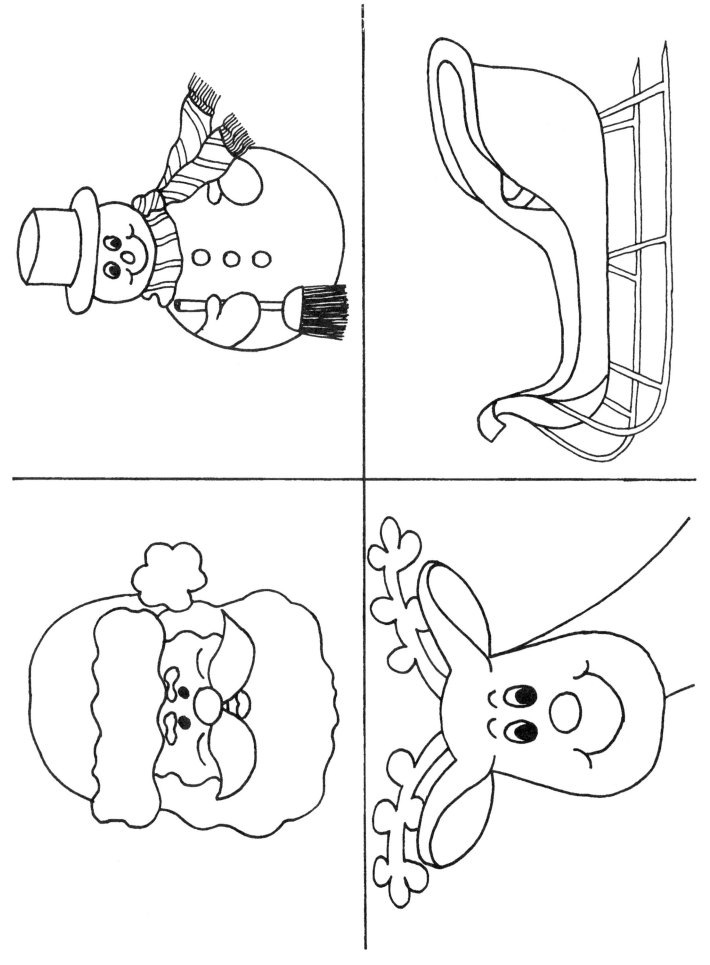

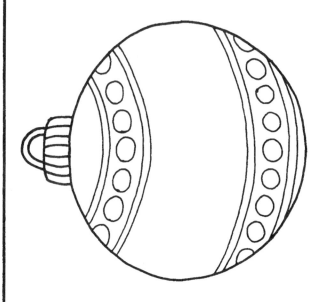

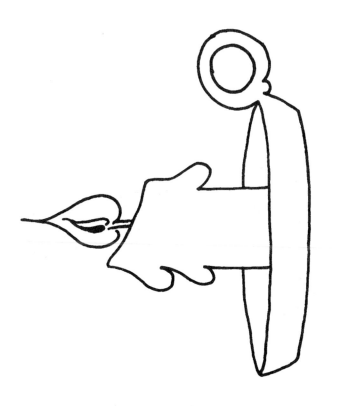

3

4

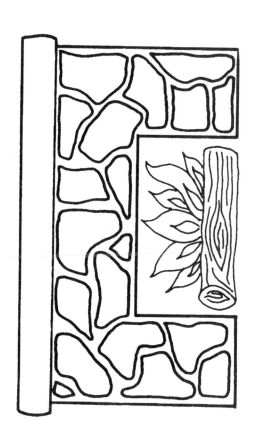

What Shall We Put On The Christmas Tree?

6

What shall we put on the
Christmas tree

to make it bright to see?

Let's put a star on the Christmas tree

to make it bright to see.

8

What shall we put on the Christmas tree

to make it bright to see?

Let's put lights on the
Christmas tree

to make it bright to see.

10

What shall we put on the Christmas tree

to make it bright to see?

Let's put garlands on the Christmas tree

Let's make it bright to see.

What shall we put on the Christmas tree

to make it bright to see?

Let's put bells on the
Christmas tree

to make it bright to see.

14

What shall we put on the Christmas tree

to make it bright to see?

Let's put an angel on the
Christmas tree

to make it bright to see.

16

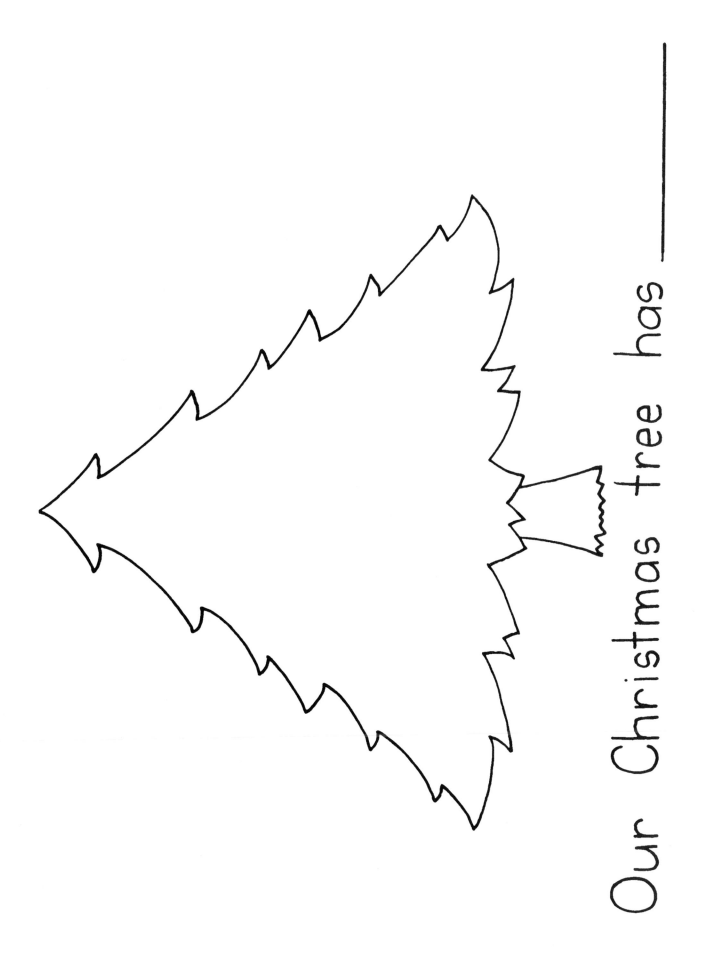

Our Christmas tree has _____

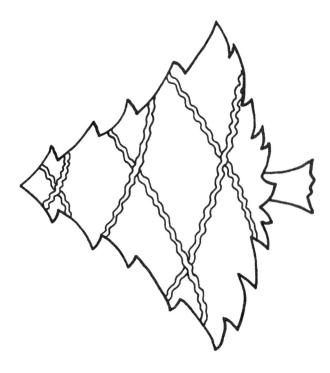

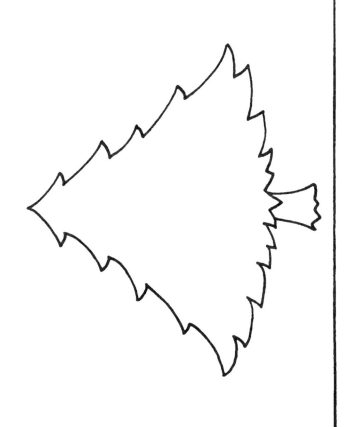

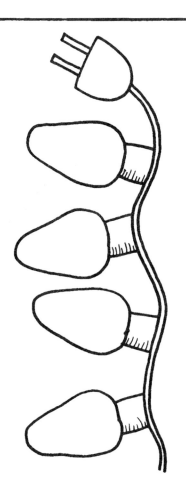

18

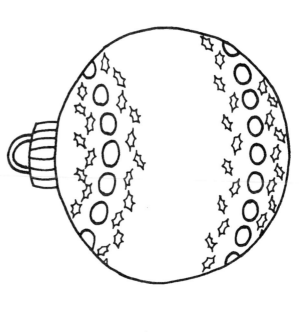

20

I like trees, trees,

_____ trees,

_____

I like trees.

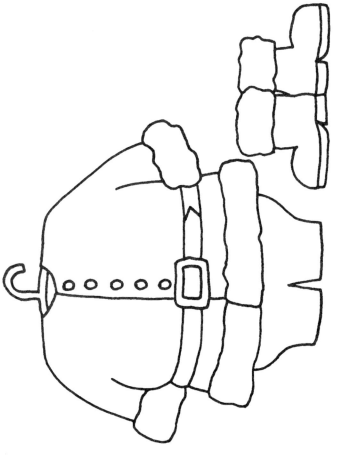

22

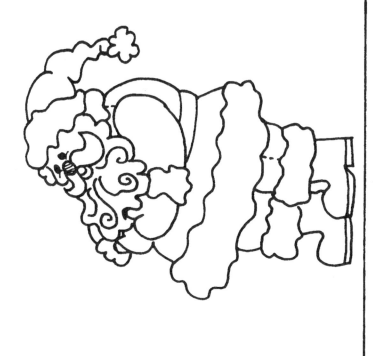

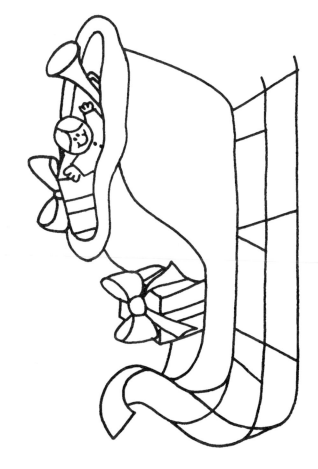

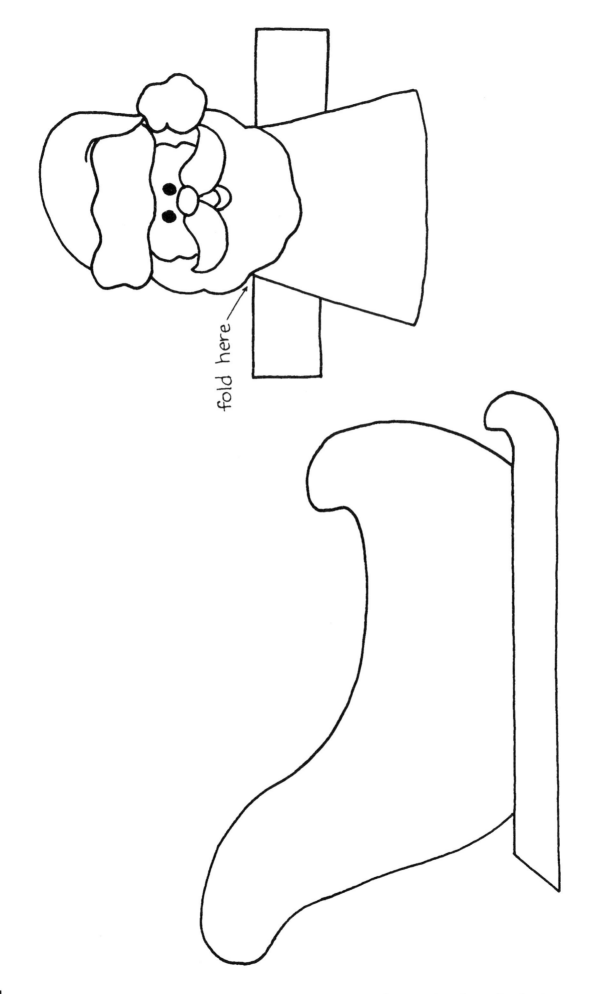

fold here

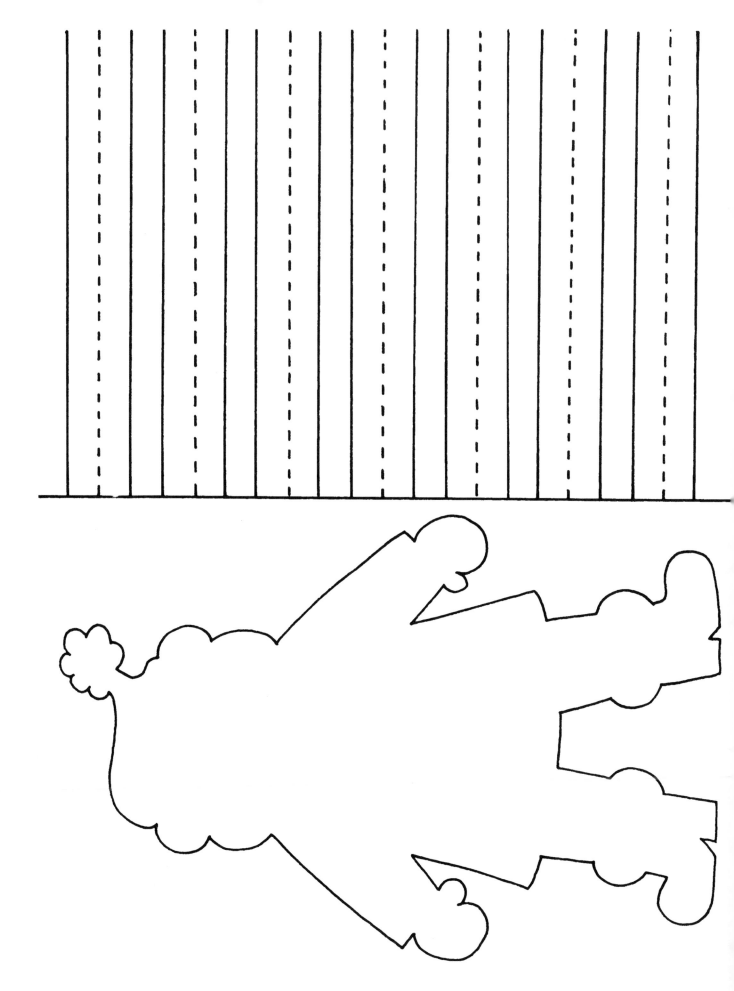

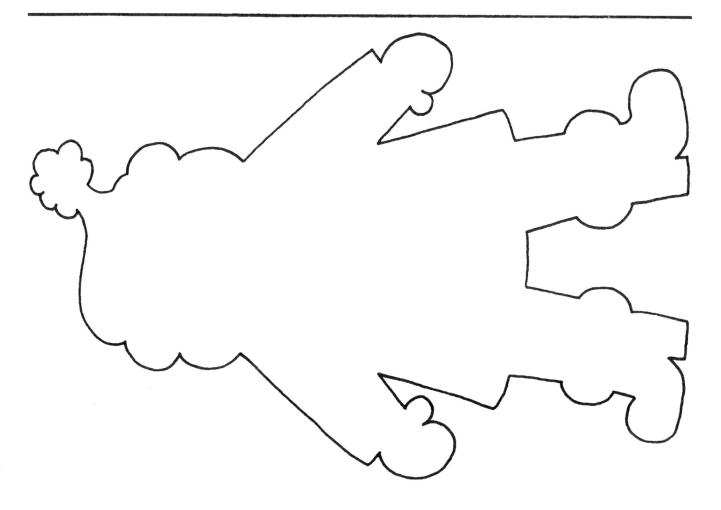

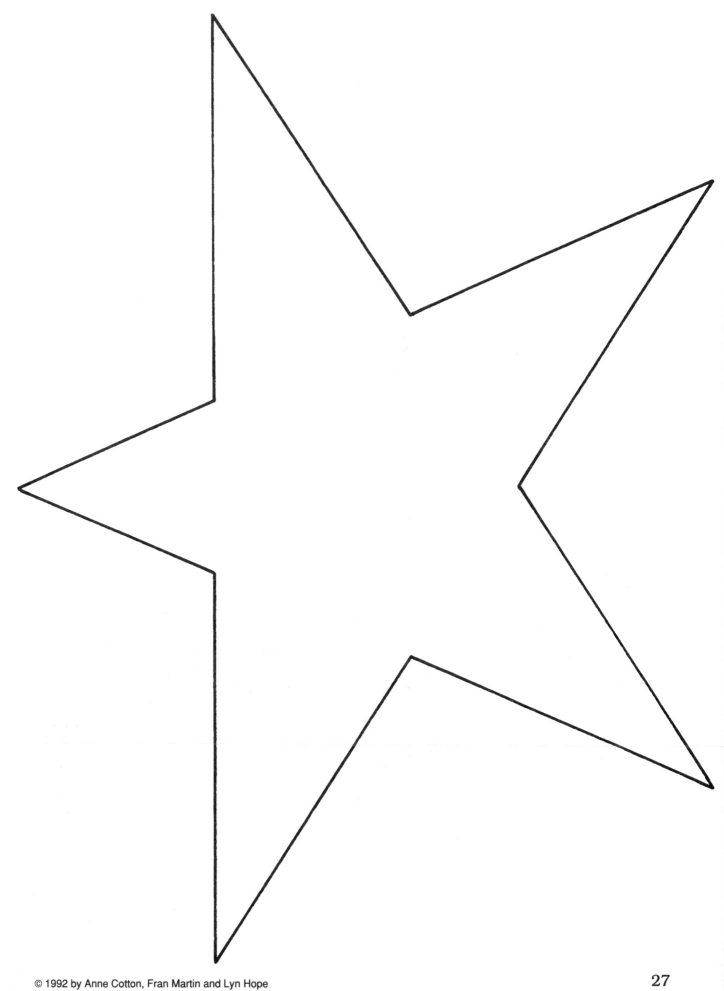

27

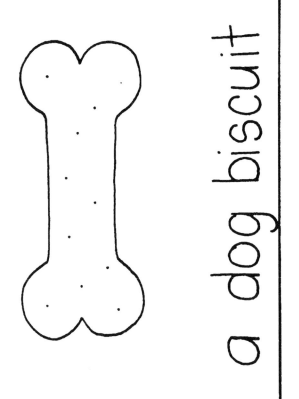

a dog biscuit

honey

dog

bear

28

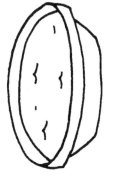

milk

oats

goat

horse

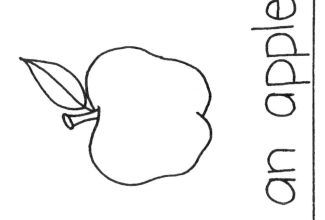

an apple

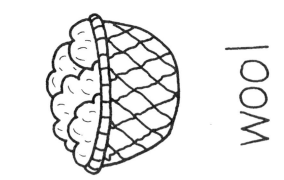

wool

pig

sheep

a worm

TRA-LA LA - LA

a song

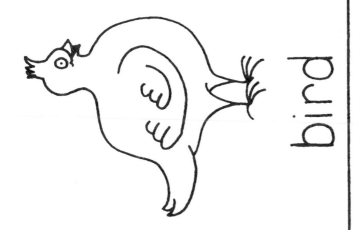

bird

bird

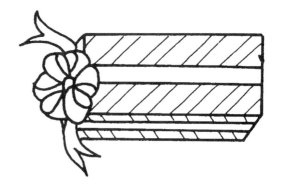

Merry Christmas

Some gifts are large,

Some gifts are small,

Some gifts are round,

Some gifts are tall,

But a gift from the heart
Is the best gift of all.

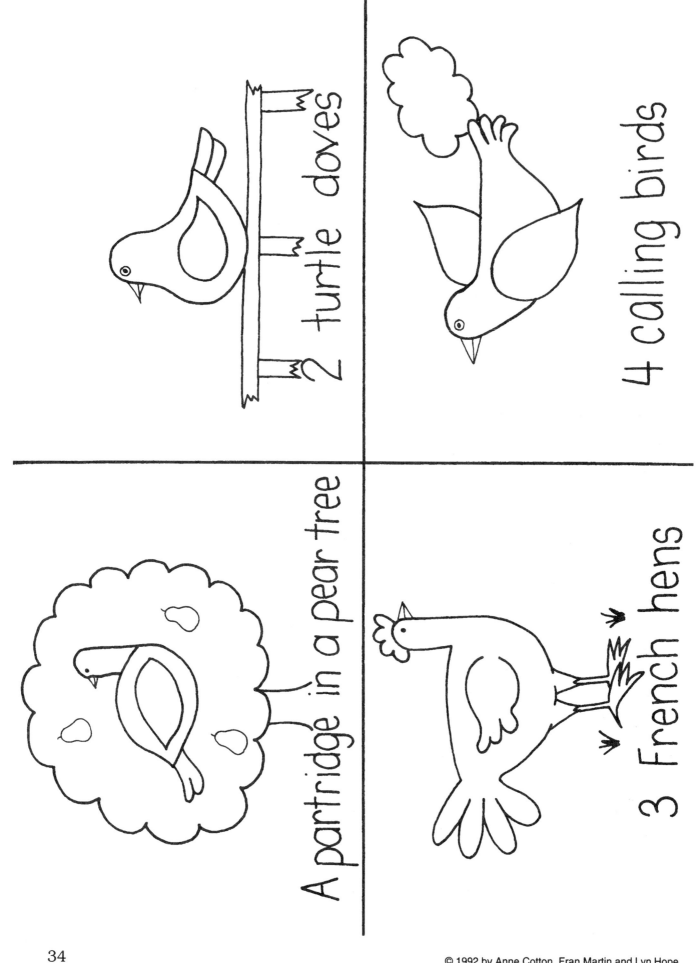

2 turtle doves

4 calling birds

A partridge in a pear tree

3 French hens

34

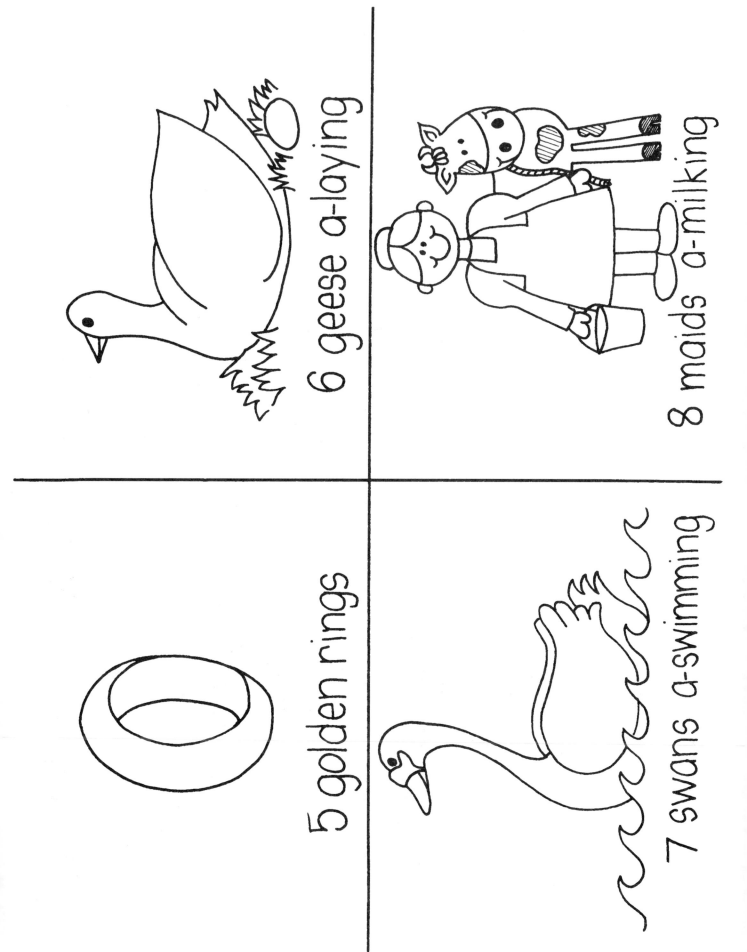

6 geese a-laying

8 maids a-milking

5 golden rings

7 swans a-swimming

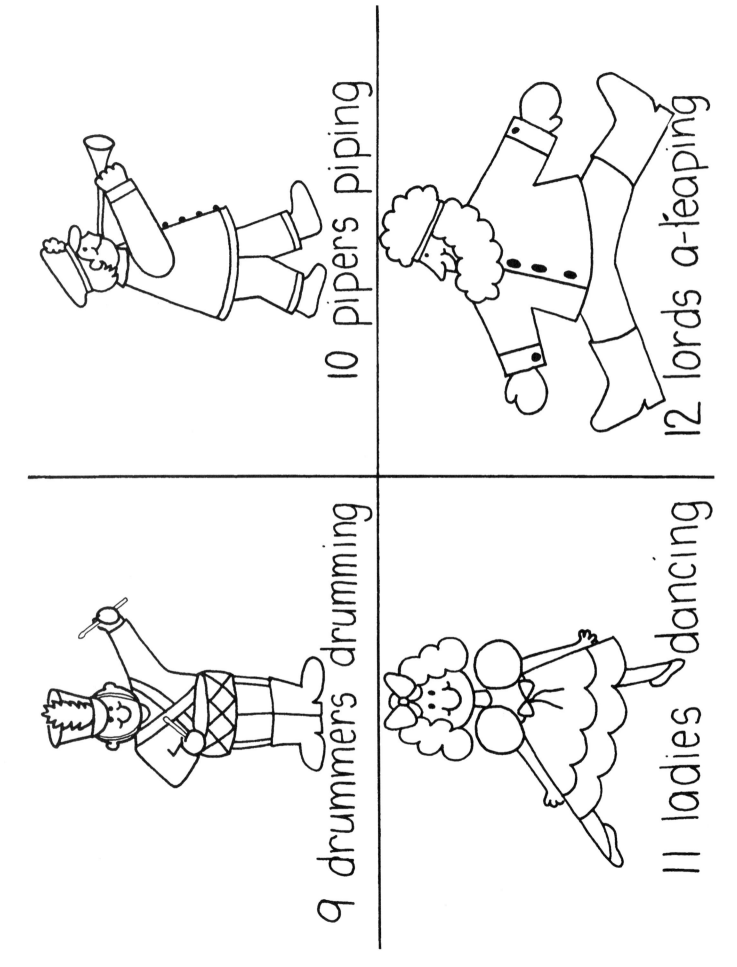

10 pipers piping

12 lords a-leaping

9 drummers drumming

11 ladies dancing

4

8

12

3

7

11

2

6

10

A

5

9

1st day	2nd day
3rd day	4th day
5th day	6th day
7th day	8th day
9th day	10th day
11th day	12th day

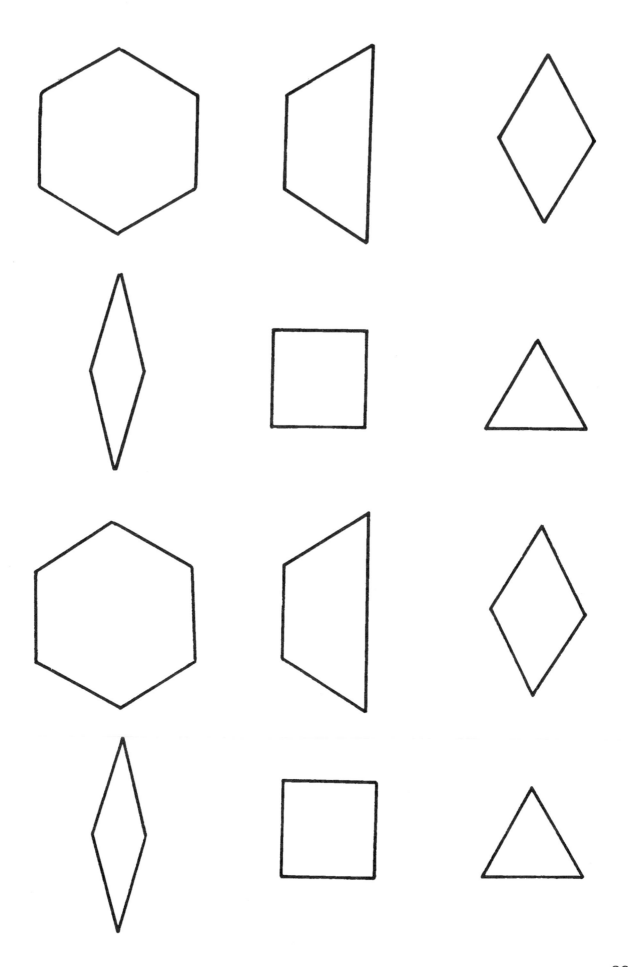

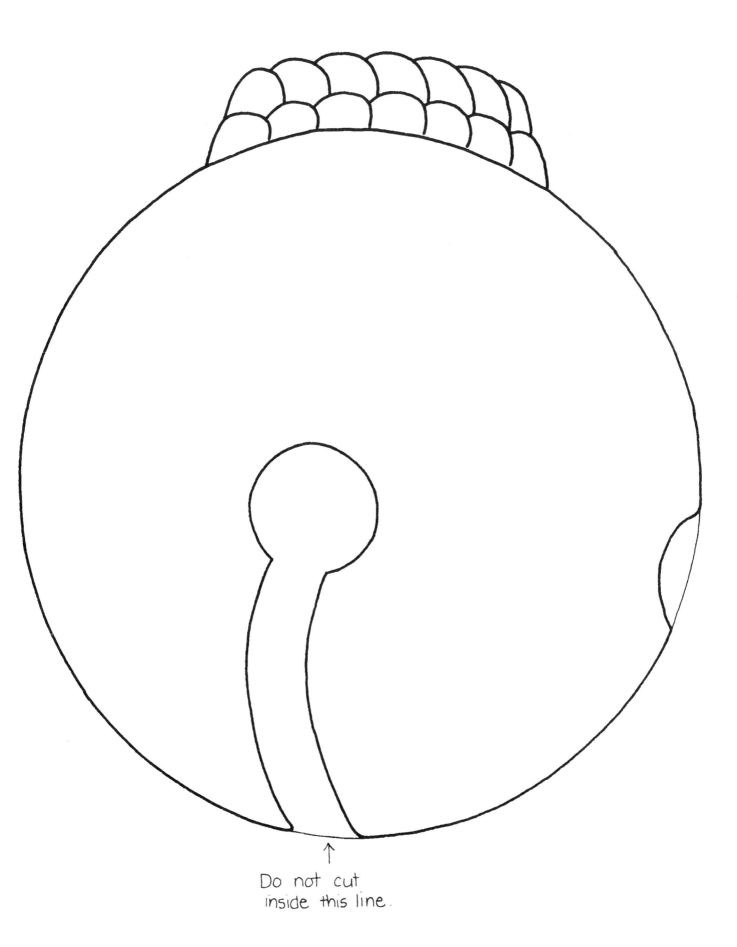

Do not cut
inside this line.

40

roof - continue pattern out to edge of 9"x12" construction paper

chimney↓

windows
Title↓

door→

A Little
House of Brown

42

44

46

48

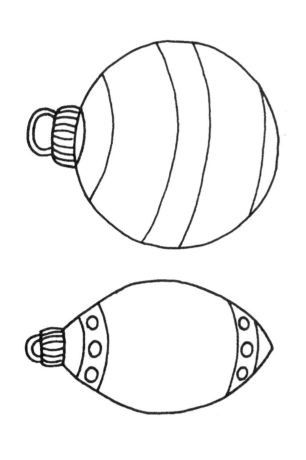

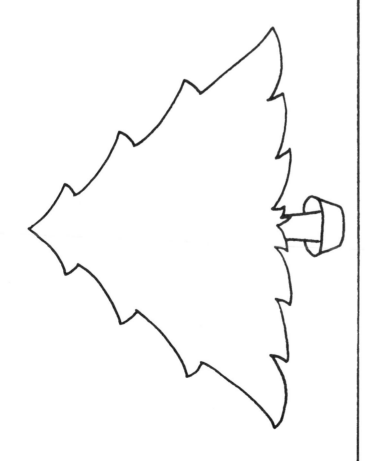

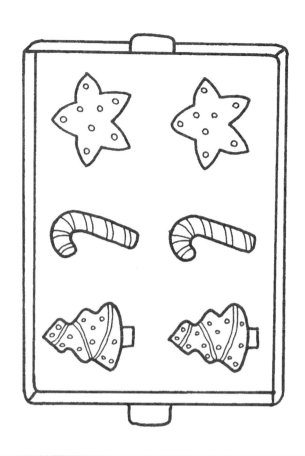

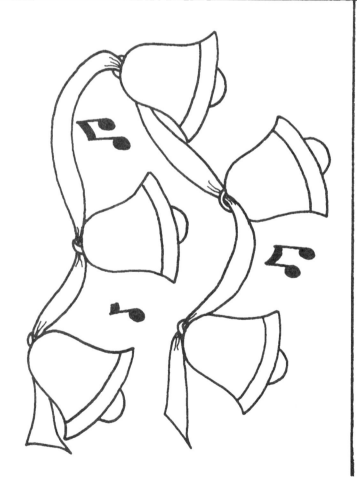

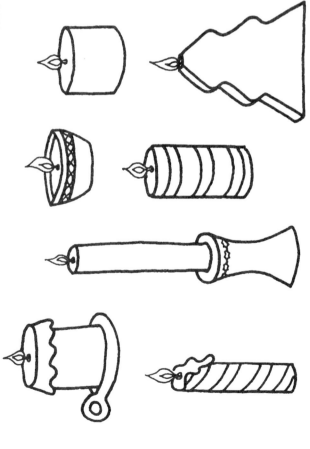

50

_____ is for _____